W9-BUQ-526

THE CHINESE HOROSCOPES LIBRARY

SNAKE

KWOK MAN-HO

DORLING KINDERSLEY
LONDON • NEW YORK • STUTTGART

A DORLING KINDERSLEY BOOK

Senior Editor		Sharon Lucas
Art Editor		Camilla Fox
Managing Editor		Krystyna Mayer
Managing Art Editor		Derek Coombes
DTP Designer		Doug Miller
Production Controller		Antony Heller

Artworks: Danuta Mayer 4, 8, 11, 17, 27, 29, 31, 33, 35;
Giuliano Fornari 21; Jane Thomson; Sarah Ponder.

Special Photography by Steve Gorton. Thank you to the Bristol City Museum & Art Gallery,
Oriental Section; The British Museum, Chinese Post Office, and The Powell-Cotton Museum.

Additional Photography: Eric Crichton, Steve Gorton, Dave King, Diana Miller, Steve Shott,
Chris Stevens, Paul Williams.

Picture Credits: Bridgeman Art Library/Oriental Museum, Durham University 15, The
British Museum 23bl, Circa Photo Library 14.

First published in Great Britain in 1994
by Dorling Kindersley Limited,
9 Henrietta Street, London WC2E 8PS

Copyright © 1994 Dorling Kindersley Limited, London
Text copyright © 1994 ICOREC

All rights reserved. No part of this publication may be reproduced, stored in a retrieval
system, or transmitted in any form or by any means, electronic, mechanical, photocopying,
recording or otherwise, without the prior permission of the copyright owner.

A CIP catalogue record for this book is available from the British Library

ISBN 0-7513-0121-3

Reproduced by GRB Editrice, Verona, Italy
Printed and bound in Hong Kong by Imago

CONTENTS

INTRODUCING CHINESE HOROSCOPES

For thousands of years, the Chinese have used their astrology and religion to establish a harmony between people and the world around them.

The exact origins of the twelve animals of Chinese astrology – the Rat, Ox, Tiger, Rabbit, Dragon, Snake, Horse, Ram, Monkey, Rooster, Dog, and Pig – remain a mystery. Nevertheless, these animals are important in Chinese astrology. They are much more than general signposts to the year, and to the possible good or bad times ahead for us all. The twelve animals of Chinese astrology are considered to be a reflection of the Universe itself.

YIN AND YANG SYMBOL
White represents the female force of yin, and black represents the masculine force of yang.

YIN AND YANG

The many differences in our natures, moods, health, and fortunes reflect the wider changes within the Universe. The Chinese believe that

every single thing in the Universe is held in balance by the dynamic, cosmic forces of yin and yang. Yin is feminine, watery, and cool; the force of the Moon and the rain. Yang is masculine, solid, and hot; the force of the Sun and the Earth. According to ancient Chinese belief, the concentrated essences of yin and yang became the four seasons, and the scattered essences of yin and yang became the myriad creatures that are found on Earth.

The twelve animals of Chinese astrology are all associated with either yin or yang. The forces of yin rise as winter approaches. These forces decline with the warmth of spring, when yang begins to assert itself. Even in the course of a normal day, yin and yang are at work, constantly changing and balancing. These forces also naturally rise and fall within us all.

Everyone has their own internal balance of yin and yang. This affects our tempers, ambitions, and health. We also respond to the changes of weather, to the environment, and to the people who surround us.

THE FIVE ELEMENTS

All that we can touch, taste, or see is divided into five basic types or elements – wood, fire, earth, gold, and water. Everything in the Universe can be linked to one of these elements.

For example, the element fire is linked to the Snake and to the Horse. This element is also linked to the colour red, bitter-tasting food, the season of summer, and the emotion

of joy. The activity of these five elements indicates the fortune that may befall us.

AN INDIVIDUAL DISCOVERY

Chinese astrology can help you balance your yin and yang. It can also tell you which element you are, and the colours, tastes, parts of the body, or emotions that are linked to your particular sign. Your fortune can be prophesied according to the year, month, day, and hour in which you were born. You can identify the type of people to whom you are attracted, and the career that will suit your character. You can understand your changes of mood, your reactions to other places, and to other people. In essence, you can start to discover what makes you an individual.

DIVINATION STICKS
Another ancient and popular method of Chinese fortune-telling is using special divination sticks to obtain a specific reading from prediction books.

CASTING YOUR HOROSCOPE

The Chinese calendar is based on the movement of the Moon, unlike the calendar used in the Western world, which is based on the movement of the Sun.

Before you begin to cast your Chinese horoscope, check your year of birth on the chart on pages 44 to 45. Check particularly carefully if you were born in the early months of the year. The Chinese year does not usually begin until January or February, and you might belong to the previous Chinese year. For example, if you were born in 1961 you might assume that you were born in the Year of the Ox. However, if your birthday falls before 15 February you belong to the previous Chinese year, which is the Year of the Rat.

THE SIXTY-YEAR CYCLE
The Chinese measure the passing of time by cycles of sixty years. The twelve astrological animals appear five times during the sixty-year cycle, and they appear in a slightly different form every time. For example, if you were born in 1953

you are a Snake on the Grass, but if you were born in 1965, you are a Snake Coming Out of the Hole.

MONTHS, DAYS, AND HOURS
The twelve lunar months of the Chinese calendar do not correspond exactly with the twelve Western calendar months. This is because Chinese months are lunar, whereas Western months are solar. Chinese months are normally twenty-nine to thirty days long, and every three to four years an extra month is added to keep approximately in step with the Western year.

One Chinese hour is equal to two Western hours, and the twelve Chinese hours correspond to the twelve animal signs.

The year, month, day, and hour of birth are the keys to Chinese astrology. Once you know them, you can start to unlock your personal Chinese horoscope.

	Water
	Earth
	Wood
	Fire

	Gold
	Yin
	Yang

CHINESE ASTROLOGICAL WHEEL
In the centre of the wheel is the yin and yang symbol. It is surrounded by the Chinese astrological character linked to each animal. The band of colour reveals your element, and the outer ring shows whether you are yin or yang.

MYTHS AND LEGENDS

*According to Chinese legend, the Jade Emperor, the ruler of
Heaven, asked to see the Earth's twelve most interesting
animals, then awarded the Snake sixth place.*

The snake is a female symbol in
China. It is respected for its great
intelligence, but it is also regarded as
treacherous. River gods were
thought to be in snake
form, and the snake
was often
worshipped.
Snake liver was
regarded for its
medicinal value,
and it is believed
that snakeskin
should never be
thrown away,
because it will
eventually bring
wealth to the
owner. Dreams of
a black snake foretell the birth of a
girl, dreams of a white or grey snake
foretell the birth of a boy, and if a man
dreams of a single snake it forecasts a
new relationship with a woman.

SMILING SNAKE
*This finely carved, ancient Chinese,
green jade snake shows the snake's
scaly markings, as well as its typically
secretive smile.*

THE UNSUCCESSFUL SNAKE
Long ago, there was an unsuccessful
snake. These creatures are usually
harbingers of death for
the Chinese, because
they appear
suddenly and
kill swiftly.
However, this
particular snake
was neither fast
nor overly
poisonous.
Although he
always tried his
best, he did not
frighten anyone.
One day, a horse
gave him a blow to
the head, leaving him unable to bite
or poison anything. The snake was
bitterly disappointed, but refused to
give up hope. "After all," he said to
himself, "just seeing a snake can

TORTOISE AND SNAKE

A snake on top of a tortoise symbolizes the direction of the north. This figure is made of bronze, and is from China's Han dynasty (206BC–AD220).

sometimes give humans a fatal heart attack." He moved to the Buddhist temple, but the old and the weak there did not pay him the slightest attention, or show the merest flicker of fear, no matter how fierce or vicious he looked.

Downcast, he decided to throw himself to his death that night off the top of the pagoda. When all was quiet and dark, the snake slowly climbed up the pagoda. He failed to notice a thief, weighed down with stolen temple treasures. Just as the the snake hurled himself suicidally from the top of the pagoda, the thief stopped. The snake landed straight onto the thief's neck.

The thief collapsed, and uttered a blood-curdling scream. The snake was stunned, but he was the hero of the hour, and the temple monks could not reward him enough. They made a snake den in the temple, brought him tasty titbits, and made his life as luxurious as possible. Unwittingly, the unsuccessful snake had found success at last.

· SNAKE ·
PERSONALITY

The appearance and manner of the Snake are refined and elegant. It is a polite and confident creature, and finds itself attracted to debate and investigation.

You tend to be found at the centre of social events, holding court with your conversational skills and your humour. You enjoy the exchange of ideas, but can easily become bored.

MOTIVATION
You are a good judge of character and opportunities. When you have set yourself a target you will not abandon it until completion.

Usually you are patient and considerate, but if you find yourself under threat you react sharply, and are prepared to take revenge.

It is important that you achieve your goals with subtlety since you do not handle confrontation or failure easily. You are always prepared to give advice but find it hard to accept it when it is offered. When you have to ease yourself out of difficult situations, you will happily use all

ENTWINED SNAKE AND TORTOISE
The snake and tortoise on this 16th-century rubbing represent the struggle between yin and yang. On the tortoise's shell are the constellations of Heaven and the eight trigrams of the I Ching.

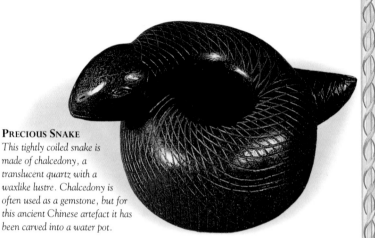

PRECIOUS SNAKE
This tightly coiled snake is made of chalcedony, a translucent quartz with a waxlike lustre. Chalcedony is often used as a gemstone, but for this ancient Chinese artefact it has been carved into a water pot.

possible means. These methods and your constant quest for success and achievements can make you seem selfish and proud. However, once you feel that your problems have been resolved and your position is safe, you should become more tranquil and understanding.

THE INNER SNAKE
You are happiest when you are immersed in deep conversation, occasionally pausing for reflection, then continuing from a new angle. You are calm and peaceful, and your friendships tend to be extremely trusting and long-term.

There is a certain mystery and depth within you that others find attractive, and you are a sensual and passionate romantic partner.

You jealously guard the people who are close to you, and take great personal care of anything that you consider important. Consequently, as a parent you are protective, understanding, and always an effective communicator.

THE SNAKE CHILD
The young Snake requires plenty of tenderness and attention, and needs to avoid tense situations or arguments.

LOVE

The Snake is seductive, passionate, and highly charismatic.
It guards its loved ones jealously, and needs to be at the
centre of its partner's life.

A combination of physical and mental attraction is extremely important in your emotional relationships. You love to exchange your ideas and interests, and once you have found your romantic match, you are an amenable, humorous, and sensitive partner.

Although you guard your partner jealously, you are also tempted to roam. Regardless of possible infidelities, however, you cling to your committed relationship, and are eager to keep your partner within your control. You enjoy attention, and always like to please, but jealous scenes make you withdraw from the intensity of romance.

Ideally, you are suited to the Ox or the Rooster. The Ox will tolerate your selfishness, and can provide you with comfort and security. The Rooster shares your interest in appearance, and you are both dependent on news, gossip, and meaningful conversations.

You are also well matched to the Rabbit, Ram, and Snake. You share the Rabbit's need

GODDESS OF LOVE
Kuan Yin is a powerful figure in Chinese mythology. Once a male Buddhist deity, she is now known as the goddess of mercy, and as Sung-tzu, the giver of children.

CHINESE COMPATIBILITY WHEEL

Find your animal sign, then look for the animals that share its background colour – the Snake has a yellow background, and is most compatible with the Rooster and the Ox. The symbol in the centre of the wheel represents double happiness.

for a safe, comfortable environment, and it will allow you to feel that you are in control. You appreciate the Ram's creativity, but the relationship could easily become too disorganized. A relationship with another Snake could prove very powerful, but you may have to spend much time apart.

You share a deep sense of respect with the Rat, but you both need to develop some

ORCHID

In China, the orchid, or Lan Hua, is an emblem of love and beauty. It is also a fertility symbol, and represents many offspring.

tolerance; the friendly Dragon will admire your wisdom; and the Pig, despite its naivety, will know how to cope with your complexities. You admire the Dog's honesty, and if you assure it of your tenderness, it will give it the space you need.

A relationship with the Tiger or the Monkey is likely to be very difficult. The Tiger is too vivacious and you are too possessive, and although the Monkey shares your intelligence, it is too fickle, and will not be controlled.

· SNAKE ·
CAREER

The Snake makes the most of its career opportunities.
It is ambitious and intelligent, but is content to relax when
it has achieved its goals.

TEACHER

The Snake is wise and astute, and
can easily turn the process of
learning into an enjoyable
experience. It is a very
charming creature,
and can inspire great
loyalty, create a happy
atmosphere, and express
its ideas with strength
and conviction. It is,
therefore, a naturally gifted teacher.
It also possesses the ability to learn from
any mistakes that it might make.

Pupil's notebook

PSYCHOLOGIST

The field of psychology could be a
rewarding arena for the Snake's
highly developed personal skills.
Juggling appeals to the Snake because
it requires an extremely deep
level of concentration.

**Juggling
balls**

Building blocks

RESTAURATEUR

Owning and running a restaurant can be a very pleasant career for the Snake. It loves to indulge itself, and has excellent taste. The Snake possesses many creative talents, and would enjoy serving beautifully presented delicacies such as smoked salmon parcels and pearly pork balls.

Smoked salmon parcels

Pearly pork balls

PHILOSOPHER

This Chinese lacquer geomancy compass would be used by a Chinese philosopher for feng shui, the ancient method of divining the hidden energy in the landscape. Such esoteric arts interest the Snake profoundly.

Geomancer's compass

Lawyer's briefcase

LAWYER

Conducting lawsuits, and advising clients on their legal rights and obligations, requires clarity of thought, a singleminded approach, and a willingness to seize opportunities. The Snake has all of these qualities, and is rarely distracted from its professional aims.

HEALTH

Yin and yang are in a continual state of flux within the body. Good health is dependent upon the balance of yin and yang being constantly harmonious.

There is a natural minimum and maximum level of yin and yang in the human body. The body's energy is known as ch'i, and is a yang force. The movement of ch'i in the human body is complemented by the movement of blood, which is a yin force. The very slightest displacement of the balance of yin or yang in the body can quickly lead to poor health. However,

LINGCHIH FUNGUS

The fungus shown in this detail from a Ch'ing dynasty bowl is the "immortal" lingchih fungus, which symbolizes longevity.

ANGELICA

This herb is widely used in Chinese medicine, and is highly regarded for its success in the treament of gynaecological disorders.

yang illness can be cured by yin treatment, and yin illness can be cured by yang treatment. Everybody has their own individual balance of yin and yang. It is likely that a hot-tempered person will have strong yang forces, and that a peaceful person will have strong yin forces. Your nature is identified with your health, and before Chinese medicine can be prescribed, your moods have to be carefully taken into account. A balance of joy, anger, sadness, happiness, worry, pensiveness, and fear must always be maintained. This fine balance is known in China as the Harmony of the Seven Sentiments.

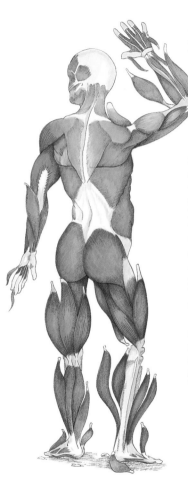

Born in the Year of the Snake, you are associated with the element fire. This element is linked with the heart, small intestine, tongue, and pulse. These are the parts of the body that are relevant to the pattern of your health. You are also associated with the emotion of joy, and with bitter-tasting food.

Angelica (*Angelica archangelica*) is associated with your Chinese astrological sign. It is prescribed to warm the spleen and stomach, restore ch'i and blood, and renew health and strength. In combination with other herbs, angelica is used to treat poor circulation, breathing difficulties, and rheumatoid arthritis. Angelica is also one of the ingredients of the "Soup to Mend Yang and Restore the Elements", which treats partial paralysis.

Chinese medicine is highly specific, therefore never take angelica or any other herb unless you are following professional advice from a fully qualified Chinese or Western doctor.

ASTROLOGY AND ANATOMY

Your element, fire, is associated with the heart and the small intestine. The heart is a yin organ, and the small intestine is a yang organ.

· SNAKE ·
LEISURE

The Snake prefers creative hobbies to active pastimes. It likes to indulge itself with life's luxuries, but will happily spend time talking, reading, or playing music.

Crystal ball

Chinese jade plaque

THE MYSTIC ARTS
Communication is one of the Snake's greatest pleasures, to the extent that it might even try to make contact with other worlds. The Snake has good taste, and would appreciate the simple mystery of this crystal ball, and the visual splendour of these Chinese tarot cards.

Chinese tarot cards

ASTROLOGY
The Snake is linked with astrology on this ancient plaque, which shows snakes and astronomical constellations.

SWIMMING

The Snake likes to be fit, but tends to avoid vigorous physical exercise. Swimming, however, does appeal, because it can be done alone, and at the Snake's own pace. It is an excellent form of exercise for posture and breathing, and intensifies the Snake's natural elegance and peaceful aura.

Goggles

Swimming caps

Trunks

ANTIQUES

The Snake is excited when it can acquire unusual objects, such as this Ch'ing dynasty bowl, which has been lovingly restored with gold to its former glory.

Auspicious Chinese fruit bowl

Archaeological trowels

ARCHAEOLOGY

The field of archaeology is an intriguing and rewarding one for the Snake. It is meticulous, and will painstakingly search for exotic artefacts.

Hand picks

· SNAKE ·
SYMBOLISM

Each astrological animal is linked with a certain food, direction, colour, emotion, association, and symbol. The Snake is also associated with the season of summer.

COLOUR

Every Chinese New Year, small red envelopes of money are handed out to children, because red is the colour of long life and good fortune. It is also the colour that is associated with the Snake.

Chinese chop print with snake

FOOD

There are five tastes according to Chinese astrology – salty, acrid, bitter, sweet, and sour. Bitter foods, such as chicory, are linked with the Snake.

Chicory

Antique Chinese compass

Hand grenades

DIRECTION
The Chinese compass points south, whereas the Western compass points north. The Snake's direction is the south.

ASSOCIATION
All forms of warfare are linked with the Snake.

Weights and spring balance

Joyful baby

SYMBOL
Weights and measures are the Snake's symbols in Chinese astrology.

EMOTION
Joy is the emotion that is connected with the Snake.

SNAKE COMING OUT OF THE HOLE

~ 1905 1965 ~

This Snake is unsure where it is going. You are associated with a bud about to break into flower, suggesting that you are on the verge of doing something.

Although you have many of the Snake's skills and attributes, sometimes you are not quite as successful as the other types of Snake. This may be because you are never quite sure what is happening.

PERSONALITY
You are likely to be popular, and to be highly respected for your trustworthiness. However, the public acclaim that others seem to receive with no effort at all could seem to pass you by. This can be frustrating, but do not allow it to become embittering.

Try to remain open, cheerful, and generous. This should always stand you in good stead, even if you sometimes feel undervalued.

The investigative aspect of the Snake is heightened in the Snake Coming Out of the Hole. You probably find it difficult, if not impossible, to relinquish issues that you feel strongly about.

This may, in part, explain why you are never likely to receive the amount of praise that you expect. You tend towards obsession, when a little distance and objectivity might prove more beneficial and impressive to other people.

No one is ever likely to doubt your sincerity, but they cannot always stay with you while you pursue an issue to the bitter end. Sometimes your obsessions can make you unsettling to live with.

FEMALE CHARACTERISTICS
Because of the calming and soothing yin influence, the female Snake Coming Out of the Hole tends to be less frustrated than the male. Considerable fame can often be

Snake Coming Out of the Hole

achieved by the female, although it is invariably ephemeral, and should never be taken for granted.

RELATIONSHIPS

In all your personal relationships, whether with your partner or your family, try to learn to give and take more. It is probably advisable for you to have children slightly later in life. This should reduce the risks of any personality clashes, and a little maturity may be just as helpful to you as to your children.

PROSPECTS

Always pursue the ideals and the issues that interest you, for it is through your drive that they will be properly addressed. Do not expect to be praised for your hard work, however. Others will invariably receive the credit, but if you really care about an issue this should not trouble you unduly. Your main concerns are with justice, and doing what is right. Remember this, and be comforted when your life seems fraught with frustration.

SNAKE IN THE FISH POND

~ 1917 1977 ~

Some Snakes feel comfortable in the water, but most do not.
You may be out of your element, but you are also stubborn,
for you are associated with a tough nail.

You are unlikely ever to give up, because you know your position in life, and accept that this is where you will stay. You will invariably try your best to make the most of it.

Life is often not easy for you, but even though you may not be doing exactly what you want to do, you are always likely to retain your innate obstinacy. This personality trait is often a strength because you rarely allow things to overcome you, but the struggle can sometimes be exhausting, too.

YOUTH

The early part of your life is likely to be fraught with struggle and difficulty, but try not to give in to your anger and frustration. Always remember the enduring image of the nail – you are personally tough and can easily survive, but you do not always have to be so obstructive.

CAREER

Luckily, all your efforts do not go unobserved. Your determination and efforts are noted by those in authority, and you are recognized as a person of integrity and value.

FRIENDSHIPS

Your obstinacy is likely to cause you some problems. Consequently, it is a good idea for you to develop the Snake characteristic of making good, long-term friends, who can offer you valuable affection and support.

FAMILY

If you are an eldest child, you will probably find that life is very much easier than if you are a second or third child. The Snake in the Fish Pond as an eldest child seems to be far more comfortable in its element, and is able to progress much further in life as a result.

Snake in the Fish Pond

RELATIONSHIPS

A committed relationship is likely to be good for you, as long as you choose a partner who is your equal. You may find that you often clash with your partner, but do not lose heart, because real affection and a mature relationship should eventually ensue.

CHILDREN

Take care with your relationship with your children, for your forceful personality may leave little room for them to develop. Try to encourage your children in their own interests, even if these are not necessarily yours. Be generous, and allow them the space to be different to you.

PROSPEROUS SNAKE

~ 1929 1989 ~

*All the best, most successful qualities of the Snake are
magnified in you. Even your name suggests that you will
always enjoy extremely good fortune.*

You are associated with blossoming and succeeding, which adds to the overall sense of auspiciousness that invariably surrounds you.

PERSONALITY

You tend to be very active and occupied. You enjoy a full social life, and become bored if there is nothing to excite or interest you.

Other people might be frustrated by a lack of stimulus, but you cope with it by becoming active. Invariably, your action leads to success in many different areas.

You have a very attractive personality, and may even become famous. Everything you do tends to turn out well, and sometimes spectacularly so. People turn to you when they want to be stimulated into thinking or acting differently. This brings you great personal satisfaction, and a good income.

FEMALE CHARACTERISTICS

Because of the yin influence, the female Prosperous Snake may sometimes suffer – her innovation and love of risk may be mistrusted by others. This should change over time, but will probably affect her early years. As an eventually successful Snake woman, she can change public prejudices, but it may be at some personal cost.

FRIENDSHIPS

All Snakes are compassionate creatures, and it is advisable for you to keep this sense of compassion running alongside your success stories. If you start bragging or boasting, rather than doing and achieving, you may find that your friends and peers turn away from you. Always remember to be kind and considerate, for you can easily afford to do so.

Prosperous Snake

PROSPECTS

Try to control your inclination towards avarice. It is a petty trait, and one that is unworthy of you. If you concentrate on the job in hand, and continue to do it well, you should easily earn the rewards that you deserve. Always remember that if you give in to temptation, and push too hard for material benefit and personal advantage, you may suffer as a consequence. If you go down unsuitable pathways and abuse your great skills, intellect, and good fortune, this would be a considerable shame. Although you might be better off financially, it would be at the expense of your integrity.

SNAKE SLEEPING
IN THE WINTER

~ 1941 2001 ~

*To sleep happily throughout the winter, this Snake must
take in an adequate amount of food to sustain itself.
Symbolically, for this Snake, food corresponds to success.*

It is very important for you to be a success. Luckily, as a Snake, success is invariably yours. You must be careful, though, for you are linked to the dead of winter, emphasizing winter's bitterness and pain.

This could mean that although you may be successful, you could also be building future problems for yourself. Do not worry too much, for if you heed this warning, you should be able to enjoy the benefits of life while avoiding the pitfalls.

PERSONALITY

You have a confusing, changeable personality. If you decide to direct all your energies towards achieving material success, you may find yourself concentrating on one side of your personality. Alternatively, if you moderate this tendency, you can probably develop another side of

yourself. At times you may oscillate between these facets of yourself – try to be consistent, for this behaviour is invariably bewildering to others.

By nature you are hardworking, very ambitious, and careful with money. In moderation, these are all admirable qualities, but try not to overwork, for this could destroy valuable relationships.

Try to keep your ambition under firm control, for this could lead you into actions of which you will later be ashamed. Even worse, these actions could also leave you with formidable enemies.

In financial matters, by all means exercise a small degree of thrift, but do not allow this to develop into a form of meanness.

Do your best to enjoy life, and remember to give yourself a treat sometimes, rather than always

Snake Sleeping in the Winter

looking to save. Try to value yourself, and your friendships and relationships, as much as, or even more than, money and success.

CAREER
At work, people in authority will probably value you as a hardworking person, and will assist your career. Beware that you do not use this influence and power to harm others, however, and make sure that you do not make your way to the top by abusing your peers.

RELATIONSHIPS
Because of the yang influence, the male Snake Sleeping in the Winter in particular needs to find an older partner. Both males and females should try to find someone older, however, to help keep their strong personalities under control.

You should enjoy a happy and rewarding partnership, but may be tempted to flirt with other people. Always try to curb these unfaithful impulses, for you will invariably hurt others, as well as yourself.

SNAKE ON THE GRASS

~ 1953 2013 ~

Restless, always wanting to go to faraway places, desperate to start new projects, and do yet more — this is the dynamic Snake on the Grass.

You are full of energy and are very clever, but this does not always lead to an easy life. It is beneficial for you to pay considerable attention to your relationship with your elders, for you are linked to ancestor worship — keeping the dead happy.

FEMALE CHARACTERISTICS

Because of the influence of the yin force, it is important for the female Snake on the Grass to pay proper attention to people in authority.

CAREER

You may find it unfair and ultimately frustrating that wealth and fame do not come straight away. To be successful, you will probably have to work very hard indeed. Always try to retain a sensible and objective outlook, and do not allow yourself to become obsessed with the pursuit of wealth and status.

The natural enthusiasm and energy that you bring to any task that interests you, and your obvious intelligence, will soon earn you the admiration of others. You may find that someone in authority begins to look after you, and furthers your career. In the future you will probably have to break free from this liaison, but it should be of great value to you at the time.

FAMILY

In your youth, you probably had a stormy relationship with your family. Perhaps they did not understand your drive, and you did not understand their caution.

You may even have considered them to be irritating, and less intelligent than you. Both you and your family will simply have to learn that the passing of time can bring a renewal of relationships.

Snake on the Grass

Your family problems will not affect your ability to form very good relationships with your partner and your children, and you should gradually be able to re-establish family links.

RELATIONSHIPS
Because you are a vivacious Snake, you are particularly prone to being flirtatious, or even unfaithful. This can be a rather disruptive tendency, so make every effort to choose a partner who can balance your energy and drive with a sense of calm and a long-term perspective.

Learn to appreciate your partner's gentle, calming influence, and do not run off to others just because they seem to be more attractive. If you concentrate on learning to live with your partner, you are likely to be happy and successful.

PROSPECTS
Financial success is likely to come later in life, but luckily, you are not overly motivated by monetary gain. Instead you enjoy the stimulation of fresh challenges, and prefer to use your intelligence and skills to encounter new ideas.

YOUR CHINESE
MONTH OF BIRTH

Find the table with your year of birth, and see where your
birthday falls. For example, if you were born on
30 August 1953, you were born in Chinese month 7.

1 You must learn to relax and to say what you feel. Do not always let other people set life's agenda.

2 You can be calm and cool, but you can also blaze up. Try to keep your temper under control.

3 You always appear to be in control, but are invariably anxious. Be truthful in your self-expression.

4 You are extremely enthusiastic. Your career will be very successful if you are your own boss.

5 You are considerate, but can be mean. Sometimes you make people uncomfortable by judging them.

6 You are very well balanced. You are capable, a pleasant colleague, and excellent company.

7 You are well liked, despite the odd disagreement. Learn to listen more, and never give up.

8 You have a good sense of humour. You take charge when necessary, but work by consensus.

9 You are determined to succeed, and refuse to be deterred. Spend more time building friendships.

10 You are popular and successful, and a figure in authority should help you to prosper.

11 Your feelings can overwhelm you, and swamp your judgement. Try to be more thoughtful.

12 You express your feelings honestly. You are adaptable, and should succeed in any situation.

* Some Chinese years contain double months:	
1917: Month 2	1941: Month 6
22 Feb – 22 March	25 June – 23 July
23 March – 20 April	24 July – 22 Aug
2001: Month 4	
23 April – 22 May	
23 May – 20 June	

1905	
4 Feb – 5 March	1
6 March – 4 April	2
5 April – 3 May	3
4 May – 2 June	4
3 June – 2 July	5
3 July – 31 July	6
1 Aug – 29 Aug	7
30 Aug – 28 Sept	8
29 Sept – 27 Oct	9
28 Oct – 26 Nov	10
27 Nov – 25 Dec	11
26 Dec – 24 Jan 1906	12

1917	
23 Jan – 21 Feb	1
* See double months box	2
21 April – 20 May	3
21 May – 18 June	4
19 June – 18 July	5
19 July – 17 Aug	6
18 Aug – 15 Sept	7
16 Sept – 15 Oct	8
16 Oct – 14 Nov	9
15 Nov – 13 Dec	10
14 Dec – 12 Jan 1918	11
13 Jan – 10 Feb	12

1929	
10 Feb – 10 March	1
11 March – 18 April	2
19 April – 8 May	3
9 May – 6 June	4
7 June – 6 July	5
7 July – 4 Aug	6
5 Aug – 2 Sept	7
3 Sept – 2 Oct	8
3 Oct – 30 Oct	9
1 Nov – 30 Nov	10
1 Dec – 30 Dec	11
31 Dec – 29 Jan 1930	12

1941	
27 Jan – 25 Feb	1
26 Feb – 27 March	2
28 March – 25 April	3
26 April – 25 May	4
26 May – 24 June	5
* See double months box	6
23 Aug – 20 Sept	7
21 Sept – 19 Oct	8
20 Oct – 18 Nov	9
19 Nov – 17 Dec	10
18 Dec – 16 Jan 1942	11
17 Jan – 14 Feb	12

1953	
14 Feb – 14 March	1
15 March – 13 April	2
14 April – 12 May	3
13 May – 10 June	4
11 June – 10 July	5
11 July – 8 Aug	6
9 Aug – 7 Sept	7
8 Sept – 7 Oct	8
8 Oct – 6 Nov	9
7 Nov – 5 Dec	10
6 Dec – 4 Jan 1954	11
5 Jan – 2 Feb	12

1965	
2 Feb – 2 March	1
3 March – 1 April	2
2 April – 30 April	3
1 May – 30 May	4
31 May – 28 June	5
29 June – 27 July	6
28 July – 26 Aug	7
27 Aug – 24 Sept	8
25 Sept – 23 Oct	9
24 Oct – 22 Nov	10
23 Nov – 22 Dec	11
23 Dec – 20 Jan 1966	12

1977	
18 Feb – 19 March	1
20 March – 17 April	2
18 April – 17 May	3
18 May – 16 June	4
17 June – 15 July	5
16 July – 14 Aug	6
15 Aug – 12 Sept	7
13 Sept – 12 Oct	8
13 Oct – 10 Nov	9
11 Nov – 10 Dec	10
11 Dec – 8 Jan 1978	11
9 Jan – 6 Feb	12

1989	
6 Feb – 7 March	1
8 March – 5 April	2
6 April – 4 May	3
5 May – 3 June	4
4 June – 2 July	5
3 July – 31 July	6
1 Aug – 30 Aug	7
31 Aug – 29 Sept	8
30 Sept – 28 Oct	9
29 Oct – 27 Nov	10
28 Nov – 27 Dec	11
28 Dec – 26 Jan 1990	12

2001	
24 Jan – 22 Feb	1
23 Feb – 24 March	2
25 March – 22 April	3
* See double months box	4
21 June – 20 July	5
21 July – 18 Aug	6
19 Aug – 16 Sept	7
17 Sept – 16 Oct	8
17 Oct – 14 Nov	9
15 Nov – 14 Dec	10
15 Dec – 12 Jan 2002	11
13 Jan – 11 Feb	12

YOUR CHINESE DAY OF BIRTH

Refer to the previous page to discover the beginning of your Chinese month of birth, then use the chart below to calculate your Chinese day of birth.

If you were born on 5 May 1905, your birthday is in the Chinese month starting on 4 May. Find 4 on the chart below. Using 4 as the first day, count the days until you reach the date of your birthday. Remember that not all months contain 31 days. You were born on day 2 of the Chinese month.

If you were born in a Chinese double month, simply count the days from the first date of the month that contains your birthday.

1	2	3	4	5	6	7
8	9	10	11	12	13	14
15	16	17	18	19	20	21
22	23	24	25	26	27	28
29	30	31				

DAY 1, 10, 19, OR 28
You are trustworthy, and set high standards, but tend to rush your projects. Try to be cautious, and do not be too self-obsessed. You may receive unexpected money, but must control your spending. You are suited to a career in the public sector or the arts.

DAY 2, 11, 20, OR 29
You are honest and popular. You need peace, but also require lively company. You are prone to outbursts of temper. You tend to enjoy life, and make the most of your opportunities. You are suited to a literary or artistic career.

DAY 3, 12, 21, OR 30
You are quick-witted, but may appear to be difficult. As a result, people may be wary of being your friend. You have a disciplined character, and fight for the truth. You are suited to careers that have a competitive element.

Day 4, 13, 22, or 31

You are very warmhearted, but also have a reserved attitude, which can sometimes make you appear unapproachable. If you try to be more outgoing and sociable, you should become more popular. You have a calm and patient manner, and are suited to a career as an academic or a researcher.

Day 5, 14, or 23

Your fiery, obstinate nature can sometimes make it difficult for you to accept suggestions or opinions from others, and your stubbornness may lead to quarrels or problems. You should be lucky with money, and may often use your profits to set up new projects. Your innate intelligence will enable you to cope with a demanding career.

Day 6, 15, or 24

You have an open, stable, and cheerful character, and enjoy an active social life. You are affectionate and emotional, and have a tendency to daydream. This can lead to confusion, and your eagerness to help others may be stifled by your indecision. Although you will never be wealthy, you should always have enough money.

Day 7, 16, or 25

You enjoy a certain amount of excitement in your life, but must learn to become more realistic and disciplined. Although you are a natural performer, you should beware of alienating your friends or colleagues. In your career, the opportunity to travel is more important to you than a good salary or a high standard of living.

Day 8, 17, or 26

You have good judgement, but should not act too quickly. Your social skills may sometimes be lacking, and you may alienate other people, so try to be more tactful. You will experience poverty, but also wealth. Your calm and determined nature is combined with a free spirit, making you best suited to self-employment.

Day 9, 18, or 27

You are happy, optimistic, and warmhearted. You keep yourself busy, and are rarely troubled by trivialities. Occasionally you quarrel unnecessarily with your friends, and it is important for you to learn to control your moods. You are particularly suited to a career as a sole director or proprietor.

YOUR CHINESE
HOUR OF BIRTH

In Chinese time, one hour is equal to two Western hours.
Each Chinese double hour is associated with one of the
twelve astrological animals.

11 P.M. – 1 A.M. RAT HOUR
You are independent and have a hot temper. Try to think before you speak. Your thrifty nature will be useful in business and at home. You are always willing to help those who are close to you, and they will return your support.

1 – 3 A.M. OX HOUR
Up to the age of twenty, your life could be difficult, but your fortunes are likely to improve after these troublesome years. In your career, be prepared to take a risk or to leave home during your youth to achieve your goals. You should enjoy a prosperous old age.

3 – 5 A.M. TIGER HOUR
You have a lively and creative nature, which may cause family arguments in your youth. Between the ages of twenty and forty you may

have many problems. Luckily, your fortunes are likely to improve dramatically in your forties.

5 – 7 A.M. RABBIT HOUR
Your parents should be helpful, but your siblings may be your rivals. You may have to move away from home to achieve your full potential at work. Your committed relationship may take time to become settled, but you should get along much better with everyone after middle age.

7 – 9 A.M. DRAGON HOUR
You have a quick-witted, determined, and attractive nature. Your life will be busy, but you could sometimes be lonely. You should achieve a good standard of living. Try to curb your excessive self-confidence, for it could make working relationships difficult.

9 – 11 A.M. SNAKE HOUR

You have a talent for business and should find it easy to build your career and provide for your family. You have a particularly generous spirit, and will gladly help your friends when they are in trouble. Unfortunately, family relationships are unlikely to run smoothly.

11 A.M. – 1 P.M. HORSE HOUR

You are active, clever, and obstinate. Try to listen to advice. You are fascinated with travel and with changing your life. Learn to control your extravagance, for it could lead to financial suffering.

1 – 3 P.M. RAM HOUR

Steady relationships with your family, friends, or partners are difficult, because you have an active nature. You are clever, but must not force your views on others. Your fortunes are likely to be at their lowest in your middle age.

3 – 5 P.M. MONKEY HOUR

You earn and spend money easily. Your character is attractive, but frustrating, too. Sometimes your parents are not able to give you adequate moral support. Your committed relationship should be good, but do not brood over emotional problems for too long – if you do your career could suffer.

5 – 7 P.M. ROOSTER HOUR

In your teenage years you may have many arguments with your family. There could even be a family division, which should eventually be resolved. You are trustworthy, kind, and warmhearted, and never intend to hurt other people.

7 – 9 P.M. DOG HOUR

Your brave, capable, hard-working nature is ideally suited to self-employment, and the forecast for your career is excellent. Try to control your impatience and vanity. The quality of your life is far more important to you than the amount of money you have saved.

9 – 11 P.M. PIG HOUR

You are particularly skilled at manual work and always set yourself the highest of standards. Although you are warmhearted, you do not like to surround yourself with too many friends. However, the people who are close to you have your complete trust. You can be easily upset by others, but are able to forgive and forget quickly.

YOUR FORTUNE IN OTHER ANIMAL YEARS

The Snake's fortunes fluctuate during the twelve animal years. It is best to concentrate on a year's positive aspects, and to take care when faced with the seemingly negative.

YEAR OF THE RAT
Your emotional affairs will go smoothly, and you should do well in your career. You may have minor money worries, but because the Year of the Rat is a good year for you, your happiness should more than compensate for these trivialities.

YEAR OF THE OX
This year is not an auspicious time to make investments, attempt to change career, or set up a new business. Be content to leave risk and speculation to other people, and concentrate on what is familiar, realistic, and available.

YEAR OF THE TIGER
Your fortunes will be mixed in the Year of the Tiger. The beginning of the year is likely to be marked with arguments and disagreements, but these are only temporary. The year should end on a happy note.

YEAR OF THE RABBIT
Disasters may seem to be confronting you in all areas of your life in the Year of the Rabbit. However, your family will provide you with an excellent place of refuge. Keep a low profile, wait patiently, and inevitably your life will improve.

YEAR OF THE DRAGON
You are susceptible to other people's lies and deceitfulness during the Year of the Dragon. As a result, your family life could become tense, strained, and difficult. Try to ignore idle gossip at all times, and do not allow it to make you feel stressed.

YEAR OF THE SNAKE
There could be many irritating difficulties for you in the Year of the Snake. However, if you remain on your guard, and choose your friends and partners wisely, you have a very good chance of being able to avoid these potential problems.

YEAR OF THE HORSE
Serious change is likely to be forced upon you through the combination of ill-health and various financial difficulties. As a result, you may find yourself abroad, perhaps escaping from your problems, or even in search of work.

YEAR OF THE RAM
Unfortunately, nothing seems to go well for you in the Year of the Ram. You are likely to have increasing difficulties in your family life and your professional life. It is best for you to be quiet and patient, and to simply wait for happier times.

YEAR OF THE MONKEY
To start with, it may seem as if this year is just as difficult as the last, because you are likely to be encountering many of the same problems. However, as the year proceeds, your fortune will change, and you should enjoy some success.

YEAR OF THE ROOSTER
This will be a good year for your family life and your professional life. Although you may encounter a few problems, they should not detract from the great opportunities that are soon to be revealed.

YEAR OF THE DOG
Emotional affairs and travel are surrounded with particularly good fortune in the Year of the Dog. There is a strong possibility that some form of illness will cause you problems this year, so try to take care of your physical and mental health.

YEAR OF THE PIG
You will enjoy many financial rewards this year. Unfortunately, there is a price to pay for this success, which could be in the form of deteriorating personal relationships. Avoid this at all costs by proceeding with caution.

YOUR CHINESE
YEAR OF BIRTH

*Your astrological animal corresponds to the Chinese year of
your birth. It is the single most important key in the quest
to unlock your Chinese horoscope.*

Find your Western year of birth in
the left-hand column of the chart.
Your Chinese astrological animal is
on the same line as your year of
birth, in the right-hand column of
the chart. If you were born in the
beginning of the year, check the

middle column of the chart carefully.
For example, if you were born in
1966, you might assume that you
belong to the Year of the Horse.
However, if your birthday falls
before 21 January, you actually
belong to the Year of the Snake.

1900	31 Jan – 18 Feb 1901	Rat
1901	19 Feb – 7 Feb 1902	Ox
1902	8 Feb – 28 Jan 1903	Tiger
1903	29 Jan – 15 Feb 1904	Rabbit
1904	16 Feb – 3 Feb 1905	Dragon
1905	4 Feb – 24 Jan 1906	Snake
1906	25 Jan – 12 Feb 1907	Horse
1907	13 Feb – 1 Feb 1908	Ram
1908	2 Feb – 21 Jan 1909	Monkey
1909	22 Jan – 9 Feb 1910	Rooster
1910	10 Feb – 29 Jan 1911	Dog
1911	30 Jan – 17 Feb 1912	Pig
1912	18 Feb – 5 Feb 1913	Rat
1913	6 Feb – 25 Jan 1914	Ox
1914	26 Jan – 13 Feb 1915	Tiger
1915	14 Feb – 2 Feb 1916	Rabbit
1916	3 Feb – 22 Jan 1917	Dragon

1917	23 Jan – 10 Feb 1918	Snake
1918	11 Feb – 31 Jan 1919	Horse
1919	1 Feb – 19 Feb 1920	Ram
1920	20 Feb – 7 Feb 1921	Monkey
1921	8 Feb – 27 Jan 1922	Rooster
1922	28 Jan – 15 Feb 1923	Dog
1923	16 Feb – 4 Feb 1924	Pig
1924	5 Feb – 23 Jan 1925	Rat
1925	24 Jan – 12 Feb 1926	Ox
1926	13 Feb – 1 Feb 1927	Tiger
1927	2 Feb – 22 Jan 1928	Rabbit
1928	23 Jan – 9 Feb 1929	Dragon
1929	10 Feb – 29 Jan 1930	Snake
1930	30 Jan – 16 Feb 1931	Horse
1931	17 Feb – 5 Feb 1932	Ram
1932	6 Feb – 25 Jan 1933	Monkey
1933	26 Jan – 13 Feb 1934	Rooster

1934	14 Feb – 3 Feb 1935	Dog	1971	27 Jan – 14 Feb 1972	Pig
1935	4 Feb – 23 Jan 1936	Pig	1972	15 Feb – 2 Feb 1973	Rat
1936	24 Jan – 10 Feb 1937	Rat	1973	3 Feb – 22 Jan 1974	Ox
1937	11 Feb – 30 Jan 1938	Ox	1974	23 Jan – 10 Feb 1975	Tiger
1938	31 Jan – 18 Feb 1939	Tiger	1975	11 Feb – 30 Jan 1976	Rabbit
1939	19 Feb – 7 Feb 1940	Rabbit	1976	31 Jan – 17 Feb 1977	Dragon
1940	8 Feb – 26 Jan 1941	Dragon	1977	18 Feb – 6 Feb 1978	Snake
1941	27 Jan – 14 Feb 1942	Snake	1978	7 Feb – 27 Jan 1979	Horse
1942	15 Feb – 4 Feb 1943	Horse	1979	28 Jan – 15 Feb 1980	Ram
1943	5 Feb – 24 Jan 1944	Ram	1980	16 Feb – 4 Feb 1981	Monkey
1944	25 Jan – 12 Feb 1945	Monkey	1981	5 Feb – 24 Jan 1982	Rooster
1945	13 Feb – 1 Feb 1946	Rooster	1982	25 Jan – 12 Feb 1983	Dog
1946	2 Feb – 21 Jan 1947	Dog	1983	13 Feb – 1 Feb 1984	Pig
1947	22 Jan – 9 Feb 1948	Pig	1984	2 Feb – 19 Feb 1985	Rat
1948	10 Feb – 28 Jan 1949	Rat	1985	20 Feb – 8 Feb 1986	Ox
1949	29 Jan – 16 Feb 1950	Ox	1986	9 Feb – 28 Jan 1987	Tiger
1950	17 Feb – 5 Feb 1951	Tiger	1987	29 Jan – 16 Feb 1988	Rabbit
1951	6 Feb – 26 Jan 1952	Rabbit	1988	17 Feb – 5 Feb 1989	Dragon
1952	27 Jan – 13 Feb 1953	Dragon	1989	6 Feb – 26 Jan 1990	Snake
1953	14 Feb – 2 Feb 1954	Snake	1990	27 Jan – 14 Feb 1991	Horse
1954	3 Feb – 23 Jan 1955	Horse	1991	15 Feb – 3 Feb 1992	Ram
1955	24 Jan – 11 Feb 1956	Ram	1992	4 Feb – 22 Jan 1993	Monkey
1956	12 Feb – 30 Jan 1957	Monkey	1993	23 Jan – 9 Feb 1994	Rooster
1957	31 Jan – 17 Feb 1958	Rooster	1994	10 Feb – 30 Jan 1995	Dog
1958	18 Feb – 7 Feb 1959	Dog	1995	31 Jan – 18 Feb 1996	Pig
1959	8 Feb – 27 Jan 1960	Pig	1996	19 Feb – 6 Feb 1997	Rat
1960	28 Jan – 14 Feb 1961	Rat	1997	7 Feb – 27 Jan 1998	Ox
1961	15 Feb – 4 Feb 1962	Ox	1998	28 Jan – 15 Feb 1999	Tiger
1962	5 Feb – 24 Jan 1963	Tiger	1999	16 Feb – 4 Feb 2000	Rabbit
1963	25 Jan – 12 Feb 1964	Rabbit	2000	5 Feb – 23 Jan 2001	Dragon
1964	13 Feb – 1 Feb 1965	Dragon	2001	24 Jan – 11 Feb 2002	Snake
1965	2 Feb – 20 Jan 1966	Snake	2002	12 Feb – 31 Jan 2003	Horse
1966	21 Jan – 8 Feb 1967	Horse	2003	1 Feb – 21 Jan 2004	Ram
1967	9 Feb – 29 Jan 1968	Ram	2004	22 Jan – 8 Feb 2005	Monkey
1968	30 Jan – 16 Feb 1969	Monkey	2005	9 Feb – 28 Jan 2006	Rooster
1969	17 Feb – 5 Feb 1970	Rooster	2006	29 Jan – 17 Feb 2007	Dog
1970	6 Feb – 26 Jan 1971	Dog	2007	18 Feb – 6 Feb 2008	Pig